EVERY
NIGHT IS FULL
OF STARS

EVERY NIGHT IS FULL OF STARS

More Meaningful Poems for Life

Chosen by

AOIBHÍN GARRIHY

eriu

First published in the UK by Eriu
An imprint of Bonnier Books UK
5th Floor, HYLO
103–105 Bunhill Row
London, EC1Y 8LZ

Owned by Bonnier Books
Sveavägen 56, Stockholm, Sweden

Twitter – @eriu_books
Instagram – @eriubooks

Hardback – 978-1-80418-383-0
Paperback – 978-1-80418-505-6
eBook – 978-1-80418-447-9

A CIP catalogue of this book is available from the British Library.

Typeset in Bodoni by Envy Design Ltd
Printed and bound in Great Britain by Clays Ltd. Elcograf S.p.A.

1 3 5 7 9 10 8 6 4 2

MIX
Paper | Supporting
responsible forestry
FSC
www.fsc.org   FSC® C018072

www.bonnierbooks.co.uk

*To John and our three little girls Hanorah,
Líobhan and Isla, with all my love x*

Contents

Introduction

When I sheepishly first took to Instagram during the lockdown of 2020 to share my own passion for poetry, I was unsure of how it might land, worried the audience and genre might 'jar'. Fast forward a few years and that same social media platform fuels my passion for poetry. It sustains it. My feed is full of poetry accounts from all over the world featuring classic and contemporary work, carefully selected and shared to the vast network to provide the healing words or the reassuring words or the hopeful words that someone, somewhere needs to hear. I click 'save'.

Similarly, I look forward to the days when I receive a push notification on my smartphone of a new poetry podcast episode to check out. A personal favourite is Frank Skinner's Poetry Podcast. I could listen to him dissect and interpret poetry all day long! In one of his earlier episodes, he describes poetry as 'an intermingling between your thoughts and the poets ... when the minimum is said to achieve the maximum'. It's his unapologetic indulgence in poetry – while making it completely accessible and relatable – that had me hooked right away.

How we consume and digest information is changing at a rapid rate and while my love of poetry was born and nurtured in a very natural way with the help of wonderful teachers in the conventional classroom and higher-level education system, my passion for poetry now is very much sustained in quite an unconventional way. I refer to these sources to give an example of how great poetry can be discovered and enjoyed in all sorts of ways and that the 'pretentious or irrelevant' stigma it might have acquired should be absolutely a thing of the past.

My mission with my first anthology was to break down the barrier some may have to poetry. I received so many messages from those who had no real grá (Irish for love) for it in school and so figured it simply wasn't for them. Deciding to give it another go, they'd picked up *Every Day is a Fresh Beginning* and discovered a brand-new appreciation (and in a lot of cases found love) for the form. It brought me so much joy to hear from those 'converts', if you will. I also had the pleasure of meeting and speaking to lots of students, young people around Ireland who have welcomed the anthology into their hearts, guided by their passionate English teachers … that felt like a cherry on top.

Another highlight of the past year was meeting poet Anne Casey. I discovered her work when compiling the previous collection of poems and have had an enormous admiration for her ever since. When I heard she was returning home to give a poetry reading in her native Miltown Malbay I was sold! Her readings. her voice, her insights, her content and context simply blew me away and reignited a poetry spark in me once again.

Which brings me on to this collection of poetry. I read a Robert Frost quote recently that read 'poetry is when emotion has found its thought and the thought has found words'. And that's exactly it. It helps us make sense, justify or perhaps validate our emotions. Sometimes it ignites or energises something in us. Some days it can feel like taking a deep nourishing breath. And some days it feels like you're in the company of an understanding companion.

Once again, I have taken such pleasure in curating this list of poems I really love. There is such a diverse selection from the classic and well-established to the contemporary and exciting new poets. The poems on these pages are the ones I revisit time and time again, the ones I regularly turn to for solace, hope, optimism, comfort and, yet again, sustenance. I promise the lines on these pages will act as a balm for the soul. Keep them close.

Every day is a school day and this poem reminds us of exactly that. Rumi believes every experience in life is in fact an opportunity to learn and grow.

Guest House

Rumi – translated from the Persian by
Coleman Barks with John Moyne

This being human is a guest house.
Every morning a new arrival.

A joy, a depression, a meanness,
some momentary awareness comes
as an unexpected visitor.

Welcome and entertain them all!
Even if they're a crowd of sorrows,
who violently sweep your house
empty of its furniture,
still, treat each guest honorably.
He may be clearing you out
for some new delight.

The dark thought, the shame, the malice,
meet them at the door laughing,
and invite them in.

Be grateful for whoever comes,
because each has been sent
as a guide from beyond.

'Mostly we don't want to harm each other' – this poem gives me such hope when I read it. Those mini moments matter.

Small Kindnesses

Danusha Laméris

I've been thinking about the way, when you walk
down a crowded aisle, people pull in their legs
to let you by. Or how strangers still say "bless you"
when someone sneezes, a leftover
from the Bubonic plague. "Don't die," we are saying.
And sometimes, when you spill lemons
from your grocery bag, someone else will help you
pick them up. Mostly, we don't want to harm each other.
We want to be handed our cup of coffee hot,
and to say thank you to the person handing it. To smile
at them and for them to smile back. For the waitress to
call us honey when she sets down the
bowl of clam chowder,
and for the driver in the red pick-up truck to let us pass.
We have so little of each other, now. So far
from tribe and fire. Only these brief moments of exchange.
What if they are the true dwelling of the holy, these
fleeting temples we make together when we say, "Here,
have my seat," "Go ahead—you first," "I like your hat."

There are a handful of 'mantras' I try to live my life by and, when the chips are down, really try to remember... A few inspired this piece.

Every Night is Full of Stars

Aoibhín Garrihy

Every night is full of stars
There's beauty, my dear, in the darkness
Not always apparent or clear to see
Yet humbling in its vastness

Like the boy who felt the thrill of the wave
Upon his board in the swell
His troubles seemingly left on the shore
As the majestic sea cast her spell

Or the overworked Dad who took some time off
To spend outdoors with his girl
As they counted the rings on the old oak tree
He thought "What a wonderful world"

So do whatever brings you joy
There will always be highs and lows
But the moments that test us are a blessing
It's then we truly grow

There's a comfort in knowing this too shall pass
We're really just passing through
We all enter and leave the very same way
So be sure to admire the view!

I once read that gratitude turns what we have into enough ... this poem written almost 100 years ago seems to echo that very same sentiment.

A Greeting

WH Davies

Good morning, Life, and all
Things glad and beautiful.
My pockets nothing hold,
But he that owns the gold,
The Sun, is my great friend,
His spending has no end.

Hail to the morning sky,
Which bright clouds measure high;
Hail to you birds whose throats
Would number leaves by notes;
Hail to you shady bowers,
And you green fields of flowers.

Hail to you women fair,
That make a show so rare
In cloth as white as milk,
Be't calico or silk:
Good morning, Life, and all
Things glad and beautiful.

I love this little poem and I think it might speak to the 'free spirits' – perhaps those who may struggle with the confines of the classroom and academia in the conventional sense. I certainly know one such little lady!

I Meant to Do My Work Today

Richard Le Gallienne

I meant to do my work today—
    But a brown bird sang in the apple tree,
And a butterfly flitted across the field,
    And all the leaves were calling me.

And the wind went sighing over the land,
    Tossing the grasses to and fro,
And a rainbow held out its shining hand—
    So what could I do but laugh and go?

I can't say I'm quite there yet but certainly heading in this direction! However this is not so much a poem about being boring, rather a poem of sheer contentment.

Being Boring

Wendy Cope

'May you live in interesting times.' – Chinese curse

If you ask me 'What's new?', I have nothing to say
Except that the garden is growing.
I had a slight cold but it's better today.
I'm content with the way things are going.
Yes, he is the same as he usually is,
Still eating and sleeping and snoring.
I get on with my work. He gets on with his.
I know this is all very boring.

There was drama enough in my turbulent past:
Tears and passion – I've used up a tankful.
No news is good news, and long may it last.
If nothing much happens, I'm thankful.
A happier cabbage you never did see,
My vegetable spirits are soaring.
If you're after excitement, steer well clear of me.
I want to go on being boring.

I don't go to parties. Well, what are they for,
If you don't need to find a new lover?
You drink and you listen and drink a bit more
And you take the next day to recover.
Someone to stay home with was all my desire
And, now that I've found a safe mooring,
I've just one ambition in life: I aspire
To go on and on being boring.

My Dad would always say 'Any day you can get out of the bed and pull up your own trousers is a good day'! This is the ultimate gratitude poem.

Victories

Joshua Seigal

So you got up and fed the cat. That's something.
You hauled one leg, then the other, out of your
pyjama bottoms, and you fought doggedly across

the rugged terrain of the landing. You wielded
your toothbrush like a club. You stood under
the shower's strafe for as long as it took

to deter the enemies under your skin, if just
for a while. You got your yourself dressed: trousers,
T-shirt, socks – the kit. You sat for a bit then went

to the shops for milk and fruit, whatever your tired
gut could take. You wrote. That's something.
Even read a bit too. You talked with your wife –

only half hearing through the hounding static,
but you talked nonetheless. You watched
some show about the Vikings. That's something.

That's something. And when the day was done
you dropped heavily into bed, your mind bulging
with a thousand tiny battles, a thousand mini victories.

This poem feels like the holidays when you are a few days in: the shoulders have finally dropped and all that concerns you is where you should sit in relation to the pool!

Serenity Prayer

Brian Bilston

Send me a slow news day,
a quiet, subdued day,
in which nothing much happens of note,
just the passing of time,
the consumption of wine,
and a re-run of *Murder, She Wrote*.

Grant me a no news day,
a spare-me-your-views day,
in which nothing much happens at all –
a few hours together,
some regional weather,
a day we can barely recall.

Brother Richard used to visit my school in Chapelizod, Dublin, when I was growing up. He would host day retreats for the students and they had an extremely profound effect on me. I love this mindset piece.

Mobile Meditation

Brother Richard

When the mobile phone
went off
right in the middle
of the meditation,
there was a wave of discomfort you
could nearly touch,
as the lady who brought it in
desperately tried to silence its
summons.
One could almost hear the inner questioning around
her:
Did you not see the no-phones sign outside?
Did you not think to check
your phone was on silent?
Though truth be told,
in the midst of the inner tutting was
another thought:
I am so glad it was not my phone that went off, and
Is my phone on silent?
How long before I should check?
Only the monk smiled
and at the end of the meditation, to
the surprise of all,
bowed to the phone owner
and thanked her

for revealing to us all
the depth of our distraction:
'Many of you were not really here,
but the ringing brought you back,
Many of you leapt to judgement, so
the ringing revealed
the real depth of your compassion.
Many of you became concerned
about your own phone going off, so
the ringing revealed the depth of
joke attachment to self.
How precious was that distraction for
what it showed you of yourself. How
precious are all distractions when they
reveal
to us how far we have travelled away
from our
practice, from our
prayer.
How precious they are, if
we consider them
to simply be
shining signposts
on the way of return,
on the way
home.'

I once heard a wise woman say, 'when you say yes to others, make sure you are not saying no to yourself'. Muriel Rukeyser seems to have it sussed too!

Yes

Muriel Rukeyser

It's like a tap-dance
Or a new pink dress,
A shit-naive feeling
Saying yes.

Some say Good morning
Some say God bless –
Some say Possibly
Some say yes.

Some say Never
Some say Unless
It's stupid and lovely
To rush into Yes.

What can it mean?
It's just like life,
One thing to you
One thing to your wife.

Some go local
Some go express
Some can't wait
To answer yes.

Some complain
Of strain and stress
The answer may be
No for Yes.

Some like failure
Some like success
Some like Yes Yes
Yes Yes Yes.

Open your eyes,
Dream but don't guess.
Your biggest surprise
Comes after Yes.

There are so many Emily Dickinson poems I would love to include in this book. This little lyric feels refreshing in an age where it seems like everybody wants to be 'somebody' and anonymity is a rare commodity.

I'm Nobody! Who are you?

Emily Dickinson

I'm Nobody! Who are you?
Are you – Nobody – too?
Then there's a pair of us!
Don't tell! they'd advertise – you know!

How dreary – to be – Somebody!
How public – like a Frog –
To tell one's name – the livelong June –
To an admiring Bog!

I was always familiar with the first two lines of this piece but only recently discovered the poem in full. In an age of cancel culture as we witness how someone can go from hero to zero seemingly overnight this poem certainly rings true.

Solitude

Ella Wheeler Wilcox

Laugh, and the world laughs with you;
Weep, and you weep alone;
For the sad old earth must borrow its mirth,
But has trouble enough of its own.
Sing, and the hills will answer;
Sigh, it is lost on the air;
The echoes bound to a joyful sound,
But shrink from voicing care.

Rejoice, and men will seek you;
Grieve, and they turn and go;
They want full measure of all your pleasure,
But they do not need your woe.
Be glad, and your friends are many;
Be sad, and you lose them all,—
There are none to decline your nectared wine,
But alone you must drink life's gall.

Feast, and your halls are crowded;
Fast, and the world goes by.
Succeed and give, and it helps you live,
But no man can help you die.
There is room in the halls of pleasure
For a large and lordly train,
But one by one we must all file on
Through the narrow aisles of pain.

In today's fickle world, Shakespeare's words feel more poignant than ever, reminding us that once we have one good friend/ally/champion it can be enough to get through the worst of times.

Sonnet 29

William Shakespeare

When, in disgrace with fortune and men's eyes,
I all alone beweep my outcast state,
And trouble deaf heaven with my bootless cries,
And look upon myself and curse my fate,
Wishing me like to one more rich in hope,
Featured like him, like him with friends possessed,
Desiring this man's art and that man's scope,
With what I most enjoy contented least;
Yet in these thoughts myself almost despising,
Haply I think on thee, and then my state,
(Like to the lark at break of day arising
From sullen earth) sings hymns at heaven's gate;

    For thy sweet love remembered such wealth brings
    That then I scorn to change my state with kings.

When I read this James Fenton piece, I instantly thought of the people I love and admire in my own life, who really know where they came from and have a very clear sense of self (warts and all!). It's the type of person I find myself instantly drawn to.

The Ideal

James Fenton

This is where I came from.
I passed this way.
This should not be shameful
Or hard to say.

A self is a self.
It is not a screen.
A person should respect
What he has been.

This is my past
Which I shall not discard.
This is the ideal.
This is hard.

Another raw and real gift from Jan Brierton celebrating our perfect imperfections. I framed this one and it's now hanging proudly in my en-suite.

Sound Body

by Jan Brierton

Dear body,

I didn't mean what I said about your wobbly bits.
I love your stretch marks and scars,
And your big droopy tits.
Your round blancmange belly and
    your two boiled-ham thighs.
I love the crepe paper creases,
Around each of your eyes.

I love the pimple that lodges
    on your forehead for weeks.
I love the hair on your toes,
and the dimples on your bum cheeks.

And though sometimes I wish
    that your legs were longer.
I'm you, you are me,
And together we're stronger.

You hold me.
You host me.
You move me around.
My body,
My gift.

Dear body,
You're sound.

Donna Ashworth's Instagram page is a balm for the soul. She is one of the poets I just love to follow online and I could have included so many of her wonderful pieces in this anthology. Here's one on perception versus reality.

Unstoppable

Donna Ashworth

Unstoppable they called her
but I saw her stop
I saw her stop
many many times.

Sometimes
I thought she had stopped
for good

but no
she always found a way
to resurrect.

To rise again.

Not the same
never the same.

Each time a little more determined
and a little less vulnerable.

Unstoppable they said
but I think
it was in the stopping

that she found
her power.

I love this poem for its nautical theme but the line "'Tis the set of a soul that decides its goal' is a very beautiful metaphor for mindset. A great reminder that, more often than not, circumstance is not the deciding factor in one's fate, rather our outlook and approach to it.

The Winds of Fate

Ella Wheeler Wilcox

One ship drives east and another drives west
With the selfsame winds that blow;
    'Tis the set of the sails
    And not the gales
That tells us the way to go.

Like the winds of the seas are the winds of fate
As we voyage along through the life;
    'Tis the set of a soul
    That decides its goal,
And not the calm or the strife.

As someone who turns to the sea for therapy, this poem is a 'hard relate'.

The Sea Question

Elizabeth Smither

The sea asks "How is your life now?"
It does so obliquely, changing colour.
It is never the same on any two visits.

It is never the same in any particular
Only in generalities: tide and such matters
Wave height and suction, pebbles that rattle.

It doesn't presume to wear a white coat
But it questions you like a psychologist
As you walk beside it on its long couch.

I couldn't leave this one out, being so close to home. It's the nostalgic scenes of a typical Irish summer for me.

The Waves at Spanish Point

Rachael Hegarty

We packed the boogie boards from the pound shop.
Pure chuffed with the sun, the long spin out
of Dublin, pulled west to the Atlantic.
We piled out of the car at Spanish Point.
The waves were something else – three, four foot high –
taunting us to come in and try our luck.
Togs on, surf leashes strapped, the pause before
a shoreline dash and we waded out, out.

I was nearly knocked off me feet, the pull
was full-moon strong, I'd to hold firm, ready
meself, hands gripped the board, the wave curled high,
I leaped on, heaved, kept the head and boogied
the surf all the way back into the shore –
only to turn and go back out for more.

It's the deep sense of place from a Victorian poet who left her home in Co Clare, Ireland as a child for Australia that makes this poem special...

West of Fanny O'Dea's

Alice Guerin Crist

You'll not find the name in geography books,
It isn't marked on the map,
Nor mentioned in atlas or history,
Yet you've heard of the place mayhap.
The fairies lurk in the boreens there,
And the scent of the black-thorn haunts the air
Where Atlantic batters the coast of Clare
'West of Fanny O'Dea's'

Now the old folk tell, in their cheerful chat
By the kitchen fire's bright glow,
Of hurling matches, or dance or fair,
Of happenings of long ago.
How the heftiest fighters came from there,
Women and men who could do and dare,
From the very heart of the heart of Clare,
West of Fanny O'Dea's.

From 'West o' Fanny's' the folk went forth,
To the uttermost parts of the earth;
And the forest fell 'neath their sturdy stroke,
The cabin rang with mirth.
They builded homes, and the faith was there
Living circles of love and prayer,
Far from the rocky coast of Clare,
West of Fanny O'Dea's.

As the old folk chat at the kitchen fire
Of doings of long ago,
The young ones smile, with a tender scorn,
At a well-worn phrase they know:
'Now many strange countries and climes there be,
And many queer names o'er land and sea,
But where in the name of geography
Is 'West of Fanny O'Dea's?'

North Clare is a place I hold dear. When a poet like Heaney describes a place like the Burren, the result is magic.

Postscript

Seamus Heaney

And some time make the time to drive out west
Into County Clare, along the Flaggy Shore,
In September or October, when the wind
And the light are working off each other
So that the ocean on one side is wild
With foam and glitter, and inland among stones
The surface of a slate-grey lake is lit
By the earthed lightning of a flock of swans,
Their feathers roughed and ruffling, white on white,
Their fully grown headstrong-looking heads
Tucked or cresting or busy underwater.
Useless to think you'll park and capture it
More thoroughly. You are neither here nor there,
A hurry through which known and strange things pass
As big soft buffetings come at the car sideways
And catch the heart off guard and blow it open.

When reading this poem I could not help but feel a deep connection to my ancestors whose livelihoods relied so heavily on the land and sea, and all the risk, hardship and tragedy that came with it.

Twilight

Henry Wadsworth Longfellow

The twilight is sad and cloudy,
   The wind blows wild and free,
And like the wings of sea-birds
   Flash the white caps of the sea.

But in the fisherman's cottage
   There shines a ruddier light,
And a little face at the window
   Peers out into the night.

Close, close it is pressed to the window,
   As if those childish eyes
Were looking into the darkness,
   To see some form arise.

And a woman's waving shadow
   Is passing to and fro,
Now rising to the ceiling,
   Now bowing and bending low.

What tale do the roaring ocean,
   And the night-wind, bleak and wild,
As they beat at the crazy casement,
   Tell to that little child?

And why do the roaring ocean,
    And the night-wind, wild and bleak,
As they beat at the heart of the mother,
    Drive the color from her cheek?

No doubt Emily was describing the English countryside that she famously pined for when away, but this poem reminds me of my own childhood, of summer evenings in the Burren, Co Clare. The landscape, the healthy sea, the evening wind. It takes me back.

The Sun Has Set

Emily Brontë

The sun has set, and the long grass now
Waves dreamily in the evening wind;
And the wild bird has flown from that old gray stone
In some warm nook a couch to find.

In all the lonely landscape round
I see no light and hear no sound,
Except the wind that far away
Come sighing o'er the healthy sea.

Celebrated as one the poet's greatest works, 'The Lake Isle of Innisfree' is one we will all remember from school days. My full appreciation for the poem came in later years, working in Dublin but yearning for the west of Ireland and the peace that comes 'dropping slow' from time spent surrounded by nature.

The Lake Isle of Innisfree

William Butler Yeats

I will arise and go now, and go to Innisfree,
And a small cabin build there, of clay and wattles
made;
Nine bean-rows will I have there, a hive for the
honey-bee,
And live alone in the bee-loud glade.

And I shall have some peace there, for peace comes
dropping slow,
Dropping from the veils of the morning to where the
cricket sings;
There midnight's all a glimmer, and noon a purple
glow,
And evening full of the linnet's wings.

I will arise and go now, for always night and day
I hear lake water lapping with low sounds by the shore;
While I stand on the roadway, or on the pavements
grey,
I hear it in the deep heart's core.

As we endeavour to do better for the planet, for ourselves and generations to follow, Anne Casey's words will ring loud and clear.

The BBC Reports

Anne Casey

for the first time
in history, manmade
materials now outweigh
all life on Earth.

I am a child of wind and rain,
stone and bog, stratified silt slipping
slowly into relentless seas,
too long gone now from the elements
that shaped me – too far
from my childhood shore – these bones
throb for home, to distance
themselves from decades
of these insatiable cliffs
of glaring glass and
crushing concrete –
floors and walls
consuming all
the wildness
that once made us.

The rain here speaks
the same language
as my own
although it falls
on altogether
foreign
terrain.

We have lost our way
of hearing
its words.

I recently heard a woman I really admire, a sustainability strategist, talking about the climate crisis. She posed the question: when the next generation asks; 'when you knew, what did you do?', what will your answer be?

Perhaps the poet here is asking herself the very same question.

I Want to Live a Little Life

Erin Hanson

I want to live a little life,
I want to live it big,
To have a place to sit and feel the sun,
A patch of dirt to dig.

I want to reacquaint myself
With how I think and feel,
To make my tea but taste it too,
Reach out and touch what's real.

I want to learn my piece of sky
Like I'll be tested on it later,
Nothing to need, no guilty greed,
No fear I should want greater.

I want to sense the seasons change,
To know the chill of June,
Read my books the way I used to do,
Create more than consume.

I want to live a little life,
I want to own my time,
I want to look back glad
To know this little life was mine.

Karen McMillan 'speaks the secrets of early mother-hood' through her collection of work shared on her social media and books of poetry and I know for so many new moms, despite the best of intentions, this will be oh so relatable!

Self-care

Karen McMillan

If only I had
the inclination
to put into action
all the books
I bought myself
on self-care.

They sit upon
that shelf there
making a mockery
of me, and my
unwashed hair.

The trouble you see
with self-care
is me
'cos I'm required
to do it, myself.

The seductive imagery, the desperate plea! Percy is pining, and what a case he puts forward here!

Love's Philosophy

Percy Bysshe Shelley

The fountains mingle with the river
    And the rivers with the ocean,
The winds of heaven mix for ever
    With a sweet emotion;
Nothing in the world is single;
    All things by a law divine
In one spirit meet and mingle.
    Why not I with thine?—

See the mountains kiss high heaven
    And the waves clasp one another;
No sister-flower would be forgiven
    If it disdained its brother;
And the sunlight clasps the earth
    And the moonbeams kiss the sea:
What is all this sweet work worth
    If thou kiss not me?

Despite dating back to early Victorian times, something about this poem feels very modern. It's the cheeky spark in that last four lines and the final one, in particular, I just love.

Rondeau

Leigh Hunt

Jenny kissed me when we met,
    Jumping from the chair she sat in;
Time, you thief, who love to get
    Sweets into your list, put that in:
Say I'm weary, say I'm sad,
    Say that health and wealth have missed me,
Say I'm growing old, but add,
    Jenny kissed me.

'Our love came unannounced' as many often do ...
when you least expect it. The beauty of this piece is
the unconditional nature of the love described, in all
its raw and real glory.

Mouthful of Forevers

Clementine von Radics

I am not the first person you loved.
You are not the first person I looked at
with a mouthful of forevers. We
have both known loss like the sharp edges
of a knife. We have both lived with lips
more scar tissue than skin. Our love came
unannounced in the middle of the night.
Our love came when we'd given up
on asking love to come. I think
that has to be part
of its miracle.
This is how we heal.
I will kiss you like forgiveness. You
will hold me like I'm hope. Our arms
will bandage and we will press promises
between us like flowers in a book.
I will write sonnets to the salt of sweat
on your skin. I will write novels to the scar
of your nose. I will write a dictionary
of all the words I have used trying
to describe the way it feels to have finally,
finally found you.

And I will not be afraid
of your scars.

I know sometimes
it's still hard to let me see you
in all your cracked perfection,
but please know:
whether it's the days you burn
more brilliant than the sun
or the nights you collapse into my lap
your body broken into a thousand questions,
you are the most beautiful thing I've ever seen.
I will love you when you are a still day.
I will love you when you are a hurricane.

This is a lump-in-throat poem for me… It's one I come back to time and time again.

If I Had Three Lives

Sarah Russell

After "Melbourne" by the Whitlams

If I had three lives, I'd marry you in two.
And the other? That life over there
at Starbucks, sitting alone, writing—a memoir,
maybe a novel or this poem. No kids, probably,
a small apartment with a view of the river,
and books—lots of books—and time to read.
Friends to laugh with; a man sometimes,
for a weekend, to remember what skin feels like
when it's alive. I'm thinner in that life, vegan,
practice yoga. I go to art films, farmers markets,
drink martinis in swingy skirts and big jewelry.
I vacation on the Maine coast and wear a flannel shirt
weekend guy left behind, loving the smell of sweat
and aftershave more than I do him. I walk the beach
at sunrise, find perfect shell spirals and study pockmarks
water makes in sand. And I wonder sometimes
if I'll ever find you.

Written in the early 1800s, Elizabeth's sonnet is a wonderful example of a woman who knows exactly what she wants and is not 'behind the door' about telling her lover! A love that will stand the test of time … no shame in that!

If Thou Must Love Me

Elizabeth Barrett Browning

If thou must love me, let it be for nought
Except for love's sake only. Do not say,
"I love her for her smile—her look—her way
Of speaking gently,—for a trick of thought
That falls in well with mine, and certes brought
A sense of pleasant ease on such a day"—
For these things in themselves, Belovèd, may
Be changed, or change for thee—and love, so wrought,
May be unwrought so. Neither love me for
Thine own dear pity's wiping my cheeks dry:
A creature might forget to weep, who bore
Thy comfort long, and lose thy love thereby!
But love me for love's sake, that evermore
Thou mayst love on, through love's eternity.

Love and life is multilayered and multifaceted with so many twists and turns along the way. Timothy Liu's short and sweet synopsis here stopped me in my tracks.

The Lovers
Timothy Liu

I was always afraid
of the next card

the psychic would turn
over for us—
                    Forgive me
for not knowing
how we were

every card in the deck.

I think this poem brilliantly captures the complexity of two people, who may know each other intimately but the unsaid remains a sweet mystery.

Between

Micheal O'Siadhail

As we fall into step I ask a penny for your thoughts.
'Oh, nothing,' you say, 'well, nothing so easily bought.'

Sliding into the rhythm of your silence, I almost forget
how lonely I'd been until that autumn morning we met.

At bedtime up along my childhood's stairway, tongues
of fire cast shadows. Too earnest, too highstrung.

My desire is endless: others ended when I'd only started.
Then, there was you: so whole-hog, so wholehearted.

Think of the thousands of nights and the shadows fought.
And the mornings of light. I try to read your thought.

In the strange openness of your face, I'm powerless.
Always this love. Always this infinity between us.

Gifted to my Mom on her significant birthday (to be read in a Clare accent!), ever the romantic is Dad. This is their love story…

Maturing Love

Eugene Garrihy

You sat behind that shining desk, with youth and
    gleaming smile,
In suit of green and shamrock badge, that tourist
    board had style.

Would you know the way to Doolin's edge, I asked
    you just by chance.
You never heard of such a place, I was on a merry
    dance.

Your beauty was too great to leave, I asked you for
    a date,
"Kincora Ballroom" says you with glee, "but we won't
    be shtaying late".

But that was back in seventy-nine, our futures
    were unsure,
But the future something up ahead, and my life
    required a cure.

You clutched my heart with all your might, and
    blended it with yours,
We set a course and hoisted sails, in hope we could
    endure.

Side by side we worked and worked, desired to do
    our best,
 Energised like birds in spring, our goal to build
    that nest.

I asked your dad for your hand, and anxious what
    he'd say,
He gave his blessing with a smile, we were wed the
    11th of May.

Without a plan the first one came, and then came
    number two,
When three arrived you said to me, that's it, we've
    lots to do.

You took such pride in rearing them, minding day
    and night,
You taught them what was right from wrong, success
    brought great delight.

You watched our three become now nine, one more
    is on the way,
With years more fun now up ahead, it's time again
    to play.

It brings you joy to help them grow, to nurture and
    to guide,
It's what you do when at your best, and brings to
    you great pride.

You're sixty now, a birdy said, to me you're just a teen,
When we first kissed in seventy-nine, you were just
    eighteen.

So here's to you my love, may you never lose that zest,
May you find contentment as you go, as maturing
    love is best.

I'm a firm believer that, when it comes to love, actions speak louder than words.

Take Love for Granted

Jack Ridl

Assume it's in the kitchen,
under the couch, high
in the pine tree out back,
behind the paint cans
in the garage. Don't try
proving your love
is bigger than the Grand
Canyon, the Milky Way,
the urban sprawl of L.A.
Take it for granted. Take it
out with the garbage. Bring
it in with the takeout. Take
it for a walk with the dog.
Wake it every day, say,
"Good morning." Then
make the coffee. Warm
the cups. Don't expect much
of the day. Be glad when
you make it back to bed.
Be glad he threw out that
box of old hats. Be glad
she leaves her shoes
in the hall. Snow will
come. Spring will show up.
Summer will be humid.

The leaves will fall
in the fall. That's more
than you need. We can
love anybody, even
everybody. But you
can love the silence,
sighing and saying to
yourself, "That's her."
"That's him." Then to
each other, "I know!
Let's go out for breakfast!"

John Keats could be described as the OG of romantic poetry... This sonnet is a snapshot, a freeze frame of that intimate moment between two people, one hopelessly in love with the other, wanting time to simply stand still. The fact that John Keats passed away from tuberculosis at 25 makes this piece all the more poignant.

Bright Star, Would I Were Stedfast as Thou Art

John Keats

Bright star, would I were stedfast as thou art—
  Not in lone splendour hung aloft the night
And watching, with eternal lids apart,
  Like nature's patient, sleepless Eremite,
The moving waters at their priestlike task
  Of pure ablution round earth's human shores,
Or gazing on the new soft-fallen mask
  Of snow upon the mountains and the moors—
No—yet still stedfast, still unchangeable,
  Pillow'd upon my fair love's ripening breast,
To feel for ever its soft fall and swell,
  Awake for ever in a sweet unrest,
Still, still to hear her tender-taken breath,
And so live ever—or else swoon to death.

Sometimes it just is what it is...

I'm Sorry

Atticus

I'm sorry
we fell out of love.
I am.
The truth is
we didn't love the same and it's not your fault
and it's not mine
it's just the truth—
and that
my love
is why I'm sorry.

It was the title of this poem that caught my attention initially. It's rare you see that word in poetry. The poem itself is beautiful and heartbreaking and perhaps happy ... all at once.

The Day of Our Divorce Hearing

Ruth Lepson

you treated me to lunch, a spaghetti place.
We had never been so kind to each other.
When you said *I'm still a slob*, we laughed.
After lunch, we stood in the parking lot.
You said, *You have the last word*
but I said, *No, I'm tired of being
the one who sums things up.
You get the last word.*
But you couldn't think of one.
So off you went to our silver car,
I to our red one.
It's three years later.
And even that's just a story now.
Lately I don't feel as if I lived with you.
But I remember our kindness that day,
when it no longer mattered.

'And we hold each other fast against entropy, the fires and the flood' … it's innate human instinct to hold and save one another. How often we forget that. I love this reminder from Tom Hirons.

In the Meantime

Tom Hirons

Meanwhile, flowers still bloom.
The moon rises, and the sun.
Babies smile and somewhere,
Against all the odds,
Two people are falling in love.

Strangers share cigarettes and jokes.
Light plays on the surface of water.
Grace occurs on unlikely streets
And we hold each other fast
Against entropy, the fires and the flood.

Life leans towards living
And, while death claims all things at the end,
There were such precious times between,
In which everything was radiant
And we loved, again, this world.

Written in the mid 19th-century, Charles MacKay's 'A Summing Up' feels incredibly poignant, even today. And in relation to the final line, to the tired eyes of a sleep deprived mother, I have to agree with him!

A Summing Up

Charles MacKay

I have lived and I have loved;
I have waked and I have slept;
I have sung and I have danced;
I have smiled and I have wept;
I have won and wasted treasure;
I have had my fill of pleasure;
And all these things were weariness,
And some of them were dreariness;
And all these things, but two things,
Were emptiness and pain:
And Love--it was the best of them;
And Sleep--worth all the rest of them,
Worth everything but Love to my spirit and my brain.
But still my friend, O Slumber,
Till my days complete their number,
For Love shall never, never return to me again!

Given the title of this anthology, it would be remiss of me not to include this fantastical poem from Robert Louis Stevenson of a child's sheer wonder and awe at the thousands of millions of stars.

Escape at Bedtime

Robert Louis Stevenson

The lights from the parlour and kitchen shone out
Through the blinds and the windows and bars;
And high overhead and all moving about,
There were thousands of millions of stars.
There ne'er were such thousands of leaves on a tree,
Nor of people in church or the Park,
As the crowds of the stars that looked down upon me,
And that glittered and winked in the dark.

The Dog, and the Plough, and the Hunter, and all,
And the star of the sailor, and Mars,
These shone in the sky, and the pail by the wall
Would be half full of water and stars.
They saw me at last, and they chased me with cries,
And they soon had me packed into bed;
But the glory kept shining and bright in my eyes,
And the stars going round in my head.

I have grown to know and love Emma through her Instagram (@this_mama_doodles) and her beautiful drawings depicting motherhood are usually accompanied by healing words for 'Mammy'.

The Boy Who Calls Me Mammy

Emma Flynn

The boy who calls me Mammy
Is asleep in my bed
Breathing sleepy snores
Beside the books that we've read

The boy who calls me Mammy
Drops a Dodi from his mouth
That I allow at bed each night
To keep the magic in this house

Because the boy who calls me Mammy
He is only three
And it won't be long before this boy
Is too big to sleep with me

So until the night comes
When that young man calls me Mam
These nights of connection beneath the stars
Remain my soul's balm

Steve is one of Ireland's truly authentic voices and I am so delighted he is featured again in this anthology. His work is so full of heart and 'Stairs' is another example of his ability to turn those mini-moments into art.

Stairs

Steve Denehan

The towel came soft and warm from the tumble dryer
she sat in her vest
her mouth full of cereal
the spoon heavy with more
watching her program
eyes wide and hungry

I draped the towel across her shoulders
she purred and cloaked it around her
instantly, magically warm
safe
'Did your Mam do this to you when you were small
    Dad?'

I am standing on the stairs
halfway up
I slip
tumble silently
arrive in my childhood
see my mother walking toward me
arms wide
a towel stretched between them
waiting for me

'She did, and maybe you can do the same for your
    children.'
she is silent
her mouth full of cereal
the spoon heavy with more
watching her program
eyes wide and hungry

she speaks again, her words clouded with munching
'But who will wrap a warm towel around you now
    Dad?'
I smile and kiss her cheek
it is enough

there are no more warm towels for me
but there are blackbirds
cobwebs twinkling in sun showers
the smell of coffee
Tom Waits in the morning
The Blue Nile in the evening
and her
it is more than enough

As I write, the children have just gone to bed and this poem is our reality! However exhausting, Annie Lighthart's depiction of this sleep-deprived phase of parenthood is really beautiful.

The Hundred Names of Love

Annie Lighthart

The children have gone to bed.
We are so tired we could fold ourselves neatly
behind our eyes and sleep mid-word, sleep standing
warm among the creatures in the barn, lean together
and sleep, forgetting each other completely in the velvet,
the forgiveness of that sleep.

Then the one small cry:
one strike of the match-head of sound:
one child's voice:
and the hundred names of love are lit
as we rise and walk down the hall.

One hundred nights we wake like this,
wake out of our nowhere
to kneel by small beds in darkness.
One hundred flowers open in our hands,
a name for love written in each one.

God could not be everywhere, therefore he made mothers.

I'll Come to You When You Call

Jessica Urlichs

I sleep on the surface now
And I'll come to you when you call
My tired eyes adjust to the dark
You're a baby after all

And even when you're not
I'll come to you when you cry
When you're standing, calling from your cot
There will be no question why

And when you're in a bigger bed
And calling down the hall
If monsters find you in your dreams
I'll come to you when you call

And when you're staying at your friends
If you suddenly feel alone
I'll come to you when you call
And I'll bring us both back home

And if the night should take a turn
No matter what you've done
I'm here, I'm here, I'm always here
I'll always be your mum

There are no limits, or confines
No schedules, and no rules
If you need me, I'll be there
I'll come to you when you call

And when you have a family
Through all the highs and lows
I'll come to you when you call
Please just pick up the phone

But for now I'll hold you in the night
You're still so very small
I hope you know, I'll always show
Because I come to you when you call.

This one brought me back to my own childhood with my sisters, and the very same scenes at bedtime... Oh, the giddiness!

The Best Medicine

Meg Cox

It must be genetic
that just lying on our backs
made me and my brother laugh.
When we had adjoining bedrooms
our mother would shout up the stairs
stop reading now and go to sleep.
Later she would shout again
stop laughing now.

Adult, I went to yoga classes
and at the end we had to lie
on our backs on our mats and relax
doing yogic breathing, but before long
I was asked to leave before that part –
disruptive to meditation.

Come to think of it
lying on my back laughing
has caused me quite a bit of trouble
in the past.

This beautiful piece encouraging empathy in our smallies is just the right amount of wholesome – and if you're looking for daily parenting inspo, this one is one for the fridge!

May We Raise Children Who Love the Unloved Things

Nicolette Sowder

May we raise children
who love the unloved things – the dandelion, the
worms & spiderlings.
Children who sense
the rose needs the thorn
& run into rainswept days
the same way they turn towards sun...

And when they're grown &
someone has to speak for those
who have no voice
may they draw upon that
wilder bond, those days of
tending tender things
and be the ones.

As a Mom of three little girls, this poem is one for the back pocket! For those going through the heartbreak (teenage) years, the opening and closing lines of this poem are gold!

Advice To a Girl

Sara Teasdale

No one worth possessing
Can be quite possessed;
Lay that on your heart,
My young angry dear;
This truth, this hard and precious stone,
Lay it on your hot cheek,
Let it hide your tear.
Hold it like a crystal
When you are alone
And gaze in the depths of the icy stone.
Long, look long and you will be blessed:
No one worth possessing
Can be quite possessed.

This one is for John, Dada to my three little girls, and my own Dad, Eugene ... the two best men I know.

Only a Dad

Edgar Albert Guest

Only a dad, with a tired face,
Coming home from the daily race,
Bringing little of gold or fame,
To show how well he has played the game,
But glad in his heart that his own rejoice
To see him come, and to hear his voice.

Only a dad, with a brood of four,
One of ten million men or more.
Plodding along in the daily strife,
Bearing the whips and the scorns of life,
With never a whimper of pain or hate,
For the sake of those who at home await.

Only a dad, neither rich nor proud,
Merely one of the surging crowd
Toiling, striving from day to day,
Facing whatever may come his way,
Silent, whenever the harsh condemn,
And bearing it all for the love of them.

Only a dad, but he gives his all
To smooth the way for his children small,
Doing, with courage stern and grim,
The deeds that his father did for him.
This is the line that for him I pen,
Only a dad, *but the best of men*.

Most will know Rudyard's poem 'If' but this one, dating back to the 1800s, is yet another example of the incredible poet he was and it still rings true today.

The Thousandth Man

Rudyard Kipling

One man in a thousand, Solomon says,
Will stick more close than a brother.
And it's worth while seeking him half your days
If you find him before the other.
Nine hundred and ninety-nine depend
On what the world sees in you,
But the Thousandth Man will stand your friend
With the whole round world agin you.

'Tis neither promise nor prayer nor show
Will settle the finding for 'ee.
Nine hundred and ninety-nine of 'em go
By your looks or your acts or your glory.
But if he finds you and you find him,
The rest of the world don't matter;
For the Thousandth Man will sink or swim
With you in any water.

You can use his purse with no more talk
Than he uses yours for his spendings,
And laugh and meet in your daily walk
As though there had been no lendings.
Nine hundred and ninety-nine of 'em call
For silver and gold in their dealings;
But the Thousandth Man he's worth 'em all,
Because you can show him your feelings.

His wrong's your wrong, and his right's your right,
In season or out of season.
Stand up and back it in all men's sight—
With that for your only reason!
Nine hundred and ninety-nine can't bide
The shame or mocking or laughter,
But the Thousandth Man will stand by your side
To the gallows-foot—and after!

I'll never forget the moment I packed away the first outfit my little girl grew out of, never to be worn by her again, as the tears rolled down my face. I think most mothers will connect with Penelope's words.

Outgrown

Penelope Shuttle

It is both sad and a relief to fold so carefully
her outgrown clothes and line up the little worn shoes
of childhood, so prudent, scuffed and particular.
It is both happy and horrible to send them galloping
back tappity-tap along the misty chill path into the past.
It is both a freedom and a prison, to be outgrown
by her as she towers over me as thin as a sequin
in her doc martens and her pretty skirt,
because just as I work out how to be a mother
she stops being a child.

That juxtaposition of wanting them to thrive while struggling to let go. A prescription poem for empty nest syndrome!

To a Daughter Leaving Home
Linda Pastan

When I taught you
at eight to ride
a bicycle, loping along
beside you
as you wobbled away
on two round wheels,
my own mouth rounding
in surprise when you pulled
ahead down the curved
path of the park,
I kept waiting
for the thud
of your crash as I
sprinted to catch up,
while you grew
smaller, more breakable
with distance,
pumping, pumping
for your life, screaming
with laughter,
the hair flapping
behind you like a
handkerchief waving
goodbye.

This Elizabeth A.I. Powell piece comes as a gentle reminder to parents to savour (and document) all you can!

On Your Twenty-First Birthday

Elizabeth A.I. Powell

You sleep here next to me,
home from college, waitressing,
not so much a child anymore,
a grown person now, tired
from work and love and the day's
exultations, celebratory champagne.
How I'd like to have
the baby you were here between us now,
so that I could show you
the marvel that you are:
See the baby toes and fingers!
See the baby God light!
So you can understand the safety
I want to keep her in,
as I pass her care now to you.

The sheer innocence and simplicity of the grandfather/ grandson relationship is captured almost effortlessly but so wonderfully in Cecil's lines.

Leave-taking

Cecil Rajendra

The only joy
Of his old age
He often said
Was his grandson

Their friendship
Straddled
Eight decades
Three generations
They laughed, played, quarreled, embraced
Watched television together
And while the rest had
Little to say to the old man
The little fellow was
A fountain of endless chatter

When death rattled
The gate at five
One Sunday morning
Took the old man away
Others trumpeted their
Grief in loud sobs
And lachrymose blubber
He never shed tear
Just waved one of his

Small inimitable goodbyes
To his grandfather
And was sad the old man
Could not return his gesture

My aunt Mary, a great lover of poetry, sent me this poem and I instantly thought of my late uncle Sean when I read it. A man full of story, humour and wit – this poem truly resonated. It can be so difficult to resign ourselves (and our loved ones) to life's hard inevitabilities.

Dirge Without Music

Edna St. Vincent Millay

I am not resigned to the shutting away of loving
    hearts in the hard ground.
So it is, and so it will be, for so it has been, time out
    of mind:
Into the darkness they go, the wise and the lovely.
    Crowned
With lilies and with laurel they go; but I am not
    resigned.

Lovers and thinkers, into the earth with you.
Be one with the dull, the indiscriminate dust.
A fragment of what you felt, of what you knew,
A formula, a phrase remains,—but the best is lost.

The answers quick and keen, the honest look, the
    laughter, the love,—
They are gone. They are gone to feed the roses.
    Elegant and curled
Is the blossom. Fragrant is the blossom. I know.
    But I do not approve.
More precious was the light in your eyes than all the
    roses in the world.

Down, down, down into the darkness of the grave
Gently they go, the beautiful, the tender, the kind;
Quietly they go, the intelligent, the witty, the brave.
I know. But I do not approve. And I am not resigned.

Anyone who has lost a four-legged friend – or indeed a pet of any kind – will know the unimaginable pain once they depart. Having lost our 'first born' Rubie earlier this year, this poem certainly spoke to me.

The Power of the Dog

Rudyard Kipling

There is sorrow enough in the natural way
From men and women to fill our day;
And when we are certain of sorrow in store,
Why do we always arrange for more?
Brothers and Sisters, I bid you beware
Of giving your heart to a dog to tear.

Buy a pup and your money will buy
Love unflinching that cannot lie—
Perfect passion and worship fed
By a kick in the ribs or a pat on the head.
Nevertheless it is hardly fair
To risk your heart for a dog to tear.

When the fourteen years which Nature permits
Are closing in asthma, or tumour, or fits,
And the vet's unspoken prescription runs
To lethal chambers or loaded guns,
Then you will find—it's your own affair—
But ... you've given your heart to a dog to tear.

When the body that lived at your single will,
With its whimper of welcome, is stilled (how still!).
When the spirit that answered your every mood
Is gone—wherever it goes—for good,
You will discover how much you care,
And will give your heart to a dog to tear.

We've sorrow enough in the natural way,
When it comes to burying Christian clay.
Our loves are not given, but only lent,
At compound interest of cent per cent.
Though it is not always the case, I believe,
That the longer we've kept 'em, the more do we grieve:
For, when debts are payable, right or wrong,
A short-time loan is as bad as a long—
So why in—Heaven (before we are there)
Should we give our hearts to a dog to tear?

Wise words from Patricia McKernon Runkle. A listening ear and an open heart are often all that's required.

When You Meet
Someone Deep in Grief

Patricia McKernon Runkle

Slip off your needs
and set them by the door.

Enter barefoot
this darkened chapel

hollowed by loss
hallowed by sorrow

its grey stone walls
and floor.

You, congregation
of one

are here to listen
not to sing.

Kneel in the back pew.
Make no sound,

let the candles
speak.

A gentle reminder in grief to live on.

When I am Dead, My Dearest

Christina Rossetti

When I am dead, my dearest,
Sing no sad songs for me;
Plant thou no roses at my head,
Nor shady cypress tree:
Be the green grass above me
With showers and dewdrops wet;
And if thou wilt, remember,
And if thou wilt, forget.

I shall not see the shadows,
I shall not feel the rain;
I shall not hear the nightingale
Sing on, as if in pain:
And dreaming through the twilight
That doth not rise nor set,
Haply I may remember,
And haply may forget.

I remember reading this poem and the nurse's retort during peak pandemic and it really struck a chord.

Crabbit Old Woman

Phyllis McCormack

What do you see, nurse, what do you see?
What are you thinking, when you look at me-
A crabbit old woman, not very wise,
Uncertain of habit, with far-away eyes,
Who dribbles her food and makes no reply
When you say in a loud voice, I do wish you'd try.
Who seems not to notice the things that you do
And forever is losing a stocking or shoe.
Who, unresisting or not; lets you do as you will
With bathing and feeding the long day is fill.
Is that what you're thinking, Is that what you see?
Then open your eyes, nurse, you're looking at me.
I'll tell you who I am as I sit here so still!
As I rise at your bidding, as I eat at your will.
I'm a small child of 10 with a father and mother,
Brothers and sisters, who loved one another-
A young girl of 16 with wings on her feet,
Dreaming that soon now a lover she'll meet,
A bride soon at 20 - my heart gives a leap,
Recalling the vows that I promised to keep.
At 25 now I have young of my own
Who need me to build a secure happy home;
A woman of 30, my young now grow fast,
Bound to each other with ties that should last;
At 40, my young sons have grown and are gone,

But my man is beside me to see I don't mourn;
At 50 once more babies play around my knee,
Again we know children, my loved one and me.
Dark days are upon me, my husband is dead,
I look at the future, I shudder with dread,
For my young are all rearing young ones of their own.
And I think of the years and the love that I've known;
I'm an old woman now and nature is cruel-
Tis her jest to make old age look like a fool.
The body is crumbled, grace and vigor depart,
There is now a stone where I once had a heart,
But inside this old carcass, a young girl still dwells,
And now and again my battered heart swells,
I remember the joy, I remember the pain,
And I'm loving and living life over again.
I think of the years all too few- gone too fast.
And accept the stark fact that nothing can last-
So open your eyes, nurse, open and see,
Not a crabbit old woman, look closer-
See Me.

A Nurse's Reply

Phyllis McCormack

What do we see, you ask, what do we see?
Yes, we are thinking when looking at thee!
We may seem to be hard when we hurry and fuss,
But there's many of you, and too few of us.

We would like far more time to sit by you and talk,
To bath you and feed you and help you to walk.
To hear of your lives and the things you have done;
Your childhood, your husband, your daughter, your son.
But time is against us, there's too much to do -
Patients too many, and nurses too few.
We grieve when we see you so sad and alone,
With nobody near you, no friends of your own.

We feel all your pain, and know of your fear
That nobody cares now your end is so near.
But nurses are people with feelings as well,
And when we're together you'll often hear tell
Of the dearest old Gran in the very end bed,
And the lovely old Dad, and the things that he said,
We speak with compassion and love, and feel sad
When we think of your lives and the joy that you've had,
When the time has arrived for you to depart,
You leave us behind with an ache in our heart.

When you sleep the long sleep, no more worry or care,
There are other old people, and we must be there.
So please understand if we hurry and fuss -
There are many of you,
And so few of us.

I came across this poem and thought what a beautiful ode to the wondrous caregivers who help the women (and men) of today 'juggle' it all. Katharine describes this honourable work so eloquently.

The Nurse

Katharine Tynan

Such innocent companionship
Is hers, whether she wake or sleep,
'Tis scarcely strange her face should wear
The young child's grave and innocent air.

All the night long she hath by her
The quiet breathing, the soft stir,
Nor knows how in that tender place
The children's angels veil the face.

She wakes at dawn with bird and child
To earth new-washed and reconciled,
The hour of silence and of dew,
When God hath made His world anew.

She sleeps at eve, about the hour
Of bedtime for the bird and flower,
When daisies, evening primroses,
Know that the hour of closing is.

Her daylight thoughts are all on toys
And games for darling girls and boys,
Lest they should fret, lest they should weep,
Strayed from their heavenly fellowship.

She is as pretty and as brown
As the wood's children far from town,
As bright-eyed, glancing, shy of men,
As any squirrel, any wren.

Tender she is to beast and bird,
As in her breast some memory stirred
Of days when those were kin of hers
Who go in feathers and in furs.

A child, yet is the children's law,
And rules by love and rules by awe.
And, stern at times, is kind withal
As a girl-baby with her doll.

Outside the nursery door there lies
The world with all its griefs and sighs,
Its needs, its sins, its stains of sense:
Within is only innocence.

I came across this piece on YouTube in a recording of Mary Dorcey herself reciting it after she shared an insight into the origin and motivation for the piece. I love it for its profound perspective.

The Breath of History

Mary Dorcey

I am not an ordinary woman.
I wake in the morning.
I have food to eat.
No one has come in the night
to steal my child, my lover.
I am not an ordinary woman.

A plum tree
blossoms outside my window,
the roses are heavy with dew.
A blackbird sits on a branch
and sings out her heart.
I am not an ordinary woman.

I live where I want.
I sleep when I'm tired.
I write the words I think.
I can watch the sky
and hear the sea.
I am not an ordinary woman.
No one has offered me life
in exchange for another's.

No one has beaten me until I fall.
No one has burnt my skin
nor poisoned my lungs.
I am not an ordinary woman.
I know where my friends live.
I have books to read,
I was taught to read.
I have clean water to drink.
I know where my lover sleeps;
she lies beside me,
I hear her breathing.
My life is not commonplace.

At night the air
is as sweet as honeysuckle
that grows along the river bank.
The curlew cries
from the marshes
far out,

high and plaintive.
I am no ordinary woman.
Everything I touch and see
is astonishing and rare —
privileged.
Come celebrate each
privileged, exceptional thing:

water, food, sleep –
the absence of pain –
a night without fear –
a morning without
The return of the torturer.

A child safe,
a mother,
a lover, a sister.
Chosen work.
Our lives are not commonplace –
any of us who read this.
But who knows –
tomorrow or the day after…
I fell all about me
the breath of history –
pitiless
and ordinary.

After Susan's 'New Every Morning' provided the title for my first anthology, *Every Day is a Fresh Beginning*, I was eager to find more pearls of wisdom from her. Here's another reminder that without hope we are merely lost.

Hope and I

Susan Coolidge

Hope stood one morning by the way,
And stretched her fair right hand to me,
And softly whispered, "For this day
I'll company with thee."

"Ah, no, dear Hope," I sighing said;
"Oft have you joined me in the morn,
But when the evening came, you fled
And left me all forlorn.

"'Tis better I should walk alone
Than have your company awhile,
And then to lose it, and go on
For weary mile on mile,"

She turned, rebuked. I went my way,
But sad the sunshine seemed, and chill;
I missed her, missed her all the day,
And O, I miss her still.

I was uncertain whether to include this poem or not in this hopeful anthology, as all analysis refers to it as a purely melancholic poem written by a helpless man in despair, but I choose to look at this great masterpiece a little differently. I think it's a stunning piece of poetry and the 'dream debate' is as good a philosophy as any to explain our time here!

A Dream Within a Dream

Edgar Allan Poe

Take this kiss upon the brow!
And, in parting from you now,
Thus much let me avow —
You are not wrong, who deem
That my days have been a dream;
Yet if hope has flown away
In a night, or in a day,
In a vision, or in none,
Is it therefore the less *gone*?
All that we see or seem
Is but a dream within a dream.

I stand amid the roar
Of a surf-tormented shore,
And I hold within my hand
Grains of the golden sand —
How few! yet how they creep
Through my fingers to the deep,
While I weep — while I weep!
O God! Can I not grasp
Them with a tighter clasp?
O God! can I not save
One from the pitiless wave?
Is *all* that we see or seem
But a dream within a dream?

The ultimate carpe diem poem … seize the day!

The Clock of Life is Wound But Once

Robert H. Smith

The clock of life is wound but once
And no man has the power
To tell just when the hands will stop
At late or early hour.

To lose one's wealth is sad indeed
To lose one's health is more,
To lose one's soul is such a loss
That no man can restore.

The present is our own,
So live love, toil with a will
Place no faith in "tomorrow,"
For the clock may then be still.

I found the use of the word 'dangerous' very interesting in this piece by D.H. Lawrence. Today it might be replaced with 'inspiring' as so many who turn their dreams into a reality are ... although I sort of love 'dangerous' too!

Dreams

D. H. Lawrence

All people dream, but not equally.
Those who dream by night in the dusty recesses of
    their mind,
Wake in the morning to find that it was vanity.

But the dreamers of the day are dangerous people,
For they dream their dreams with open eyes,
And make them come true.

We hear the word success and successful all the time ... usually in the context of career, notoriety and wealth. I love how this piece reframes the concept and reminds us of all the meaningful ways in which we can truly succeed in life.

What is Success?

Ralph Waldo Emerson

To laugh often and much;

To win the respect of intelligent people
and the affection of children;

To earn the appreciation of honest critics
and endure the betrayal of false friends;

To appreciate beauty;
To find the best in others;

To leave the world a bit better, whether by
a healthy child, a garden patch
or a redeemed social condition;

To know even one life has breathed
easier because you have lived;

This is to have succeeded.

Index of First Lines

Acknowledgements

The editor and publisher gratefully acknowledge permission to reproduce the following copyright poems in this book:

Donna Ashworth: 'Unstoppable They Called Her' from *Life* by Donna Ashworth, 2022.

Brian Bilston: 'Serenity Prayer' by Brian Bilston from *Alexa, What is There to Know About Love?*, Picador, 2021. Reproduced with permission of the Licensor through PLSClear.

Jan Brierton: 'Sound Body' © Jan Brierton, 2023. Reproduced by kind permission of Jan Brierton.

Wendy Cope: 'Being Boring' from *If I Don't Know* by Wendy Cope, 2001, Faber and Faber Ltd.

Meg Cox: 'The Best Medicine' by Meg Cox. *Looking Over My Shoulder at Sodom* (Grey Hen Press, imprint Hen Run, 2014).